INVESTIGATING

DEMONS, POSSESSIONS, AND EXORCISMS

BY SUSAN R. GREGSON

Consultant:
Dr. Andrew Nichols
Director of the
American Institute of Parapsychology
~~~asville, Georgia

PSTONE PRESS
capstone imprint

Velocity is published by Capstone Press,
151 Good Counsel Drive, P.O. Box 669, Mankato, Minnesota 56002.
www.capstonepub.com

Books published by Capstone Press are manufactured with paper containing at least 10 percent post-consumer waste.

Library of Congress Cataloging-in-Publication Data
Gregson, Susan R.
  Investigating demons, possessions, and exorcisms / by Susan R. Gregson.
    p. cm.—(Unexplained phenomena)
  Summary: "Covers the topic of demon possession and exorcism, including history, specific cases, and skeptical arguments against the belief in demons"—Provided by publisher.
  Includes bibliographical references and index.
  ISBN 978-1-4296-4815-8 (library binding)
  1. Demonology—Juvenile literature. 2. Demoniac possession—Juvenile literature. 3. Exorcism—Juvenile literature. I. Title. II. Series.
  BF1543.G74 2011
  133.4'2—dc22   2010036927

Editorial Credits
Mandy Robbins, editor; Matt Bruning, designer; Marcie Spence, media researcher;
    Laura Manthe, production specialist

Photo Credits
Art Resource: Scala, 14-15; Bridgeman Art Library, The: Ken Welsh, 22; Getty Images, Inc.: Evening Standard, 40-41 (bottom); H. Ed Cox: 18-19; Newscom: World History Archive, 8-9; Shutterstock: Alexey Stiop, 6, algabafoto, 34 (middle), Andre Nantel, 35 (top), Andrea Leone, 34 (top), Andrei Nekrassov, 16, Apollofoto, 23 (bottom), arabi babakhanians, 7 (cells), bayberry, 35 (middle), Bershadsky Yuri, 38-39 (fire), Bliznetsov, 42-43, 44 (top left and top right), bocky, 30-31 (clouds), clearviewstock, 11 (stars), Cre8tive Images, 28 (bottom), Daniel Wiedemann, 20 (lamp), dundanim, 32-33, fotograaf limburg, 44 (top middle), Gelinshu, 34 (bottom), Galyna Andrushko, 20 (desert), Georgios Alexandris, 12-13, Gina Sanders, 32 (left), hektor2, 4-5, iDesign, 26 (bottom), 28-29 (top), iladm, 10 (desert), Ilja Masik, 44 (flames), Inka Photo Image, 10 (mushrooms), Ioan Nicolae, 31 (top), iofoto, 30 (top), Ivan Cholakov Gostock-dot-net, cover (top), Jason Stitt, 21 (bottom both), Jose AS Reyes, 36-37, kbrowne41, 17 (left), krovacevic, 13 (bottom), Kurhan, 5 (top), 26 (top), LANBO, 42 (brain), Laurin Rinder, 45, Leah-Anne Thompson, 24-25, Maree Stachel-Williamson, 5 (bottom), MarkauMark, 36 (stamp), Michael Felix Photography, 44 (gargoyle), Mikhail, cover (bottom), motorolka, 39 (middle), Mykhaylo Palinchak, 30-31 (woman), Noam Armonn, 23 (top), Pakimon, 41 (top), Pefkos, 41 (middle), Richard A. McGuirk, 17 (middle), Richard Griffin, 11 (crystal), ronstik, 38 (tape), Sebastian Kaulitzki, 23 (middle), Skazka Grez, 29 (middle), Slava Gerj, 10 (top), Stacy Barnett, 35 (bottom), Steve Shoup, 25 (top), Tanya Len, 7 (woman), Utemov Alexy, 4 (books), Ventura, 21 (top), Wayne Johnson, 17 (right), Yuri Arcurs, 29 (bottom)

Printed in the United States of America in Stevens Point, Wisconsin.
092010
005934WZS11

TABLE OF CONTENTS

POSSESSED?

In 2007 an American woman believed she was being attacked by demons. The woman wanted to keep her identity a secret. She went by the false name of Julia.

Dr. Richard E. Gallagher was one of several doctors Julia saw to see if her problems had medical causes. Gallagher claimed that he witnessed Julia acting very strangely. He saw no reasonable explanation for these events. Gallagher believed Julia was **possessed** by demons.

Gallagher claimed Julia floated inches above the floor. He said books and other objects fell off nearby shelves around her.

possessed	having one's mind and body taken over

According to Gallagher and other witnesses, Julia spoke in different languages. But she had only learned to speak English. Julia also spoke with a deep voice that sounded nothing like her. The voice shouted, "Go away! She is ours!"

Julia was also said to have unusual strength while possessed. She would go into violent fits. It took several people to hold her down.

Eventually Julia received an **exorcism** from Catholic priests. After the exorcism, Julia's symptoms were lessened. But they did not entirely go away. Was Julia really possessed by a demon? Or could there be other explanations?

| **exorcism** | a religious ritual that is supposed to cast out a demon from a person's mind or body |

WHAT IS A DEMON?

To those who believe in them, a demon is an evil spirit. Demons are not a new idea. Stories of demons have been around for thousands of years. Early paintings and folklore show images and tell stories of demon possessions.

People who believe in demons have exorcisms performed to get rid of them. An exorcist performs the exorcism. This person is usually a religious leader. The exorcist orders the demon to leave in the name of God.

FACT

The word "demon" comes from the ancient Greek word *daimon*. It means "full of wisdom."

A SKEPTICAL VIEW

Some people believe in demons. But others say there is no scientific proof to back up these beliefs. In most cases, **skeptics** say people are not possessed, but sick. Some illnesses cause people to act in ways that make them look possessed. Other skeptics think that people claiming to be possessed want attention.

Today science can explain many of the symptoms of possession. But where did the belief in demons come from in the first place? Why do some people still believe in them? And what is going on when there is no scientific explanation for the symptoms of possession?

skeptic	a person who questions things that other people believe in

CHAPTER 2

DEMONS AND POSSESSION THROUGHOUT HISTORY

The idea of being possessed calls frightening visions to mind. But not all possessions have been seen as negative. In ancient times, people believed being possessed by good spirits caused **divine** visions. Some people claimed to become possessed so spirits could speak through them.

ANCIENT VISIONS

More than 3,000 years ago, the Greeks built the shrine of Delphi. The Greeks built Delphi around a spring they thought was the center of the world. A priestess, called an oracle, lived at the shrine. People traveled great distances to visit the Oracle at Delphi. They believed she could get information from the spirit world. She answered people's questions about the future.

divine   to do with or from a god

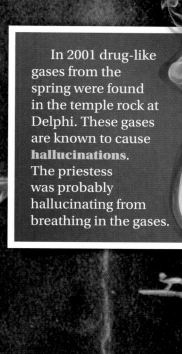

In 2001 drug-like gases from the spring were found in the temple rock at Delphi. These gases are known to cause **hallucinations**. The priestess was probably hallucinating from breathing in the gases.

FACT

Oedipus was a character in one of William Shakespeare's plays. He consulted the Oracle at Delphi.

hallucination something seen or heard that is not really there

ASK THE SHAMAN

Almost every ancient culture had a type of **shaman**. Native American shamans are probably the most well-known examples. People often asked advice of a shaman.

People believed that shamans had divine visions and could be possessed by good spirits. Shamans advised generals about when to go to war. They told kings when to sign treaties. They also gave people advice about when to plant crops or who to marry. Some cultures still have shamans today.

FACT

Some shamans believed that allowing spirits to possess them gave them special power.

Today we know that many shamans weren't having divine visions at all. They often ate special mushrooms or took drugs that made them hallucinate.

shaman	a religious or spiritual leader

For thousands of years, people have believed that crystals held special **psychic** powers. Between AD 500 and 1500, the crystal ball became a popular tool for fortune-telling in European countries. Fortune-tellers would gaze into crystal balls and claim to see visions. In the visions, fortune-tellers said they received information about a person's past, present, or future.

Some people continue to seek guidance from the spirit world. Mediums and psychics are people who claim to have knowledge of the spirit world. Some claim to know hidden information about you or your life's path. According to skeptics, all mediums and psychics are fakes.

psychic   having the ability to sense, see, or hear things that others do not

From ancient times, people have looked for positive guidance from the spirit world. But they also believed demons caused most of the world's problems. Demons were said to cause comets, volcanic eruptions, and eclipses. Some people believed demons were the reason for all illnesses. Demons had to be cast out before a person could get well. Basically, anything negative that people didn't understand was blamed on demons.

400s BC: HIPPOCRATES CASTS OUT DEMONS

About 2,400 years ago, the Greek doctor Hippocrates tried to disprove the belief in demons. He said that sickness was not caused by demons. Instead he said the body and mind could become ill. Hippocrates believed that all illness was caused by an imbalance of four different types of fluids in the body.

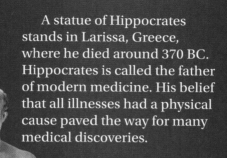

A statue of Hippocrates stands in Larissa, Greece, where he died around 370 BC. Hippocrates is called the father of modern medicine. His belief that all illnesses had a physical cause paved the way for many medical discoveries.

THE HIPPOCRATIC OATH

Throughout history, doctors have sworn the Hippocratic Oath. The words of the oath have been rewritten many times. They reflect current understanding of science and medicine. They also reflect the culture in which they're used. In ancient Greece, doctors swore dedication to the Greek gods. Today some medical schools have their own versions of the Hippocratic Oath. New doctors vow to serve their patients to the best of their abilities.

THE MIDDLE AGES

By AD 500, the Greek and Roman empires had fallen. Education declined. Without a scientific understanding of the world, people's beliefs in demons resurfaced.

The Middle Ages lasted from about 500 to 1500. During this time, anyone acting strangely was accused of being possessed.

Religious leaders had the most power during the Middle Ages. They believed demons existed and had to be cast out with prayer. If this did not work, then people were tortured. Torture was meant to make the body too uncomfortable for the demon to stay there. Unfortunately, many people died being tortured. If torture didn't work, "possessed" people were killed.

SUPERSTITION IN THE COLONIES

Supernatural beliefs didn't end with the Middle Ages. European colonists brought their beliefs with them when they settled the American colonies.

In the winter of 1692, in Salem, Massachusetts, eight young girls began acting strangely. They spoke but made no sense. They shook uncontrollably and had odd sensations on their skin. Many people thought the girls were under the spell of witches. The girls accused several people of being witches. Eventually, 20 men and women were accused of being witches and put to death. Today some researchers believe that the girls were poisoned by a fungus called ergot. It can be found in rye grain. Ergot poisoning can cause hallucinations, uncontrollable shaking, and strange skin sensations.

supernatural	describes something that cannot be given a logical explanation

1600-1700s

By the 1600s and 1700s, educated people had become more interested in science and medicine again. Science had revealed the causes of natural events once blamed on demons. By the 1700s, doctors understood many illnesses that caused symptoms of possession. Still many people had a hard time letting go of the old beliefs.

CHAPTER 3

DEMONS FROM AROUND THE WORLD

Thousands of stories exist about demons from cultures around the world. The stories usually reflect the lifestyles and concerns of those who believed in them.

MYTHICAL MERMAIDS

One demon found in folklore in many cultures was the mermaid. She was said to be part beautiful woman and part sea creature. The demon mermaid is not like the sweet ones found in children's books or movies. Demon mermaids were said to crush sailors to death or drown them. Then they would eat the sailors with their sharp teeth.

According to legend, mermaids sat upon rocks, combing their long hair and singing beautifully. A mermaid's beautiful voice attracted sailors to their doom.

Little Mermaid statue in Copenhagen, Denmark

Hundreds of years ago, sailors probably made up stories about mermaids. Instead of mermaids, the sailors probably saw seals sunning on rocks. They could have watched sharp-toothed sharks or manatees swimming in the water. It would have been easy to make up stories combining the animals into one mysterious creature. Also, there were few female sailors. Some men probably daydreamed about beautiful women.

SHARK

SEAL

MANATEE

IMAGE MAKEOVER

Hans Christian Andersen published *The Little Mermaid* in 1837. The mermaid in his story was nothing like a demon mermaid. Andersen's mermaid falls in love with a prince and wants to become human. Since Andersen wrote this fairy tale, mermaids have received a new image. Today they are usually shown as kind and helpful.

THE WINDIGO: A FLESH-EATING DEMON

The story of the Windigo demon comes from Native American tribes in the northern United States and Canada. The Hudson Bay diaries were records kept by fur trappers in the 1700s. These documents mention the demon often. The folklore of the Ojibwa, Cree, and Algonquian Indians explains that the Windigo were once humans. Somehow, they turned into possessed **cannibals**. People feared these demons most during the winter months when food was hard to find.

The Windigo supposedly roams frozen northern areas looking for humans to eat. According to legend, the Windigo **paralyzes** its victims with a scream. Then it kills and eats them. Blizzards swirl around this giant as it travels from victim to victim. It is said to be as tall as the trees of the forest.

The belief in the Windigo reflects the fears of Native Americans in that area. Long, cold winters made life difficult and food hard to come by. In the worst conditions, people may have had to choose between cannibalism and starvation. But a fear of becoming a Windigo stopped people from committing that horrible act. Lack of food can also cause people to hallucinate. It is possible that starving people hallucinated about Windigos.

cannibal	a person who eats other people
paralyze	to make someone or something helpless or unable to function

By the 1900s, doctors had recognized a mental disorder called Windigo psychosis. This disorder was found mostly in Canadian Indians who believed in the Windigo.

People with this disorder had overwhelming desires to eat humans. But they were also very afraid of becoming cannibals.

FACT

The word "windigo" comes from a Native American word that means "he eats greedily."

DEMONIC DJINN

From the forests of Canada, we go to the deserts of Arabia. According to folklore, the desert is home to the Djinn. Legend has it that there are as many Djinn as there are grains of sand. These invisible demons are said to live for centuries. Djinn appear as genies in many Arabic folktales. They live in magic lamps and grant wishes to people who rub the lamps.

Djinn were blamed for many human experiences. These include clumsiness, yawning, and nightmares. Djinn were even blamed for insanity and death. Today we know that none of these occurrences have anything to do with demons. However, scientists are still not sure why we yawn.

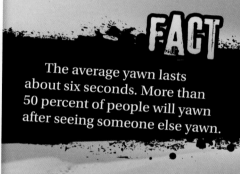

FACT

The average yawn lasts about six seconds. More than 50 percent of people will yawn after seeing someone else yawn.

Djinn were also said to cause bad weather. Believers blamed Djinn for sandstorms, whirlwinds, and shooting stars.

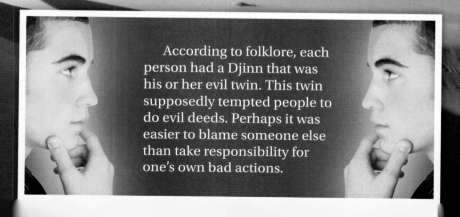

According to folklore, each person had a Djinn that was his or her evil twin. This twin supposedly tempted people to do evil deeds. Perhaps it was easier to blame someone else than take responsibility for one's own bad actions.

THE DEMON OF CHILDBIRTH

The Al is a demon whose origins come from Armenia. Armenia was once part of the Soviet Union. Hundreds of years ago, Armenians believed that Als attacked pregnant women and their unborn babies. The demon was blamed for miscarriages, stillborn babies, and death in childbirth. But the Al's power didn't stop once a child was born. According to folklore, Als could kill children up to seven months old.

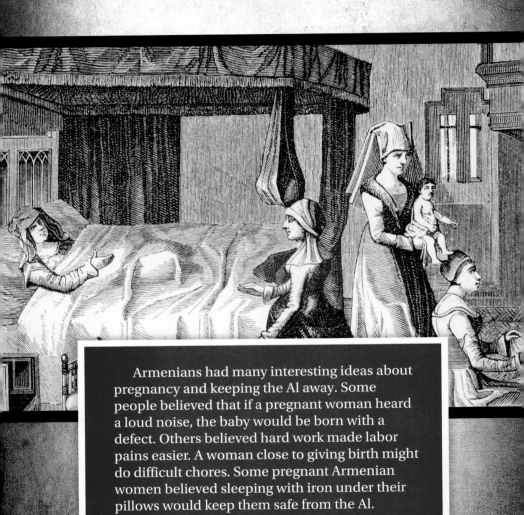

Armenians had many interesting ideas about pregnancy and keeping the Al away. Some people believed that if a pregnant woman heard a loud noise, the baby would be born with a defect. Others believed hard work made labor pains easier. A woman close to giving birth might do difficult chores. Some pregnant Armenian women believed sleeping with iron under their pillows would keep them safe from the Al.

The belief in the AI stemmed from fears of childbirth and childhood in the past. Childbirth was painful and dangerous. Hundreds of years ago, the death of a mother or child was very common. Death before the age of five was also common. The only explanation that made sense to people was that a demon was at fault. Through advances in science, we now know what was really going on.

People did not know about germs until the late 1800s. Before that time, doctors and midwives didn't wash their hands before delivering babies. Their dirty hands unknowingly caused deadly infections. Even after doctors began washing their hands, childbirth was still deadly. Mothers died from too much bleeding.

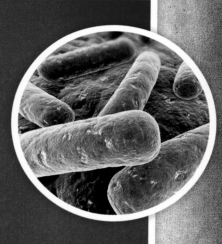

Babies often died from infection, injuries from delivery, and blocked births. A blocked birth is when the baby is turned sideways. This position stops them from being able to come out of the birth canal.

CHAPTER 4

SCIENCE EXPLAINS SYMPTOMS

Demonic possession reports decreased in the 1700s and 1800s. Scientific discoveries began to explain some of the "demonic" activities of the past. The symptoms of some illnesses are strange and alarming. Without medical knowledge, it's no wonder people long ago believed demons were the cause.

EPILEPSY

In the past, the symptoms of epilepsy were often seen as signs of possession. Epilepsy causes **seizures**. Seizures happen when a burst of electricity affects the brain. They can last from a few seconds to a few minutes.

seizure	a sudden shaking spasm that may include other uncomfortable symptoms

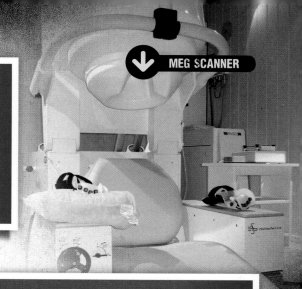

MEG SCANNER

The brains of people with epilepsy act differently than those without it. Doctors use brain scanners such as MEG scanners to detect epilepsy.

Seizures can have many symptoms. These include loss of consciousness and violent shaking. Other less common symptoms include blank stares, smacking lips, and jerky movements of the arms and legs.

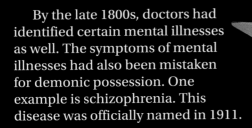

By the late 1800s, doctors had identified certain mental illnesses as well. The symptoms of mental illnesses had also been mistaken for demonic possession. One example is schizophrenia. This disease was officially named in 1911.

SCHIZOPHRENIA SYMPTOMS:

delusions	having false beliefs about something, even if physical evidence disproves these beliefs
hallucinations	seeing, hearing, smelling, tasting, and feeling things that are not there
disorganized speech	speaking in a way that is confusing or makes no sense
catatonic behavior	stiffening up one's body to the point where the person cannot move
lack of emotion	not being able to enjoy activities that one usually enjoys; lack of interest in life
physical and mental fatigue	having low energy, slow thinking, and a hard time understanding others

FREUD'S THEORIES

In the early 1900s, Dr. Sigmund Freud developed new theories of mental illness. According to Freud's theories, the human mind is a balance of three parts.

The id is made up of all of a person's **unconscious** desires. The id only cares about what a person wants and needs. Freud thought that all human behavior was driven by the desires of the id.

The ego is the logical part of the human mind. It uses reason to balance the needs of the id with appropriate behavior.

The superego is also called the conscience. The superego tells a person what is morally wrong or right.

Freud believed many symptoms of mental illness could be relieved. Patients just had to deal with the underlying mental problems.

FACT

One fourth of all adults have a mental illness.

unconscious	describes a thought a person has without being aware of it

ANXIETY AND DEPRESSION

Anxiety and depression are two of the most common mental illnesses. About 18 percent of adults suffer from anxiety at some point in their lives. Almost seven percent of adults deal with major depression. These illnesses probably caused many reports of "possession" in the past.

Many symptoms of anxiety and depression overlap with symptoms of possession. Most noticeably, those who suffer from anxiety and depression feel very unhappy. Other common symptoms include excessive crying and an inability to sleep.

- LOW MOOD
- LOW ENERGY
- OVERLY SAD
- INABILITY TO SLEEP

- SWEATING
- HEART POUNDING
- DIZZINESS
- FEELING CONFUSED
- FEAR OF INSANITY

PANIC ATTACKS

Anxiety disorders are more than just a feeling of nervousness. They often cause panic attacks. Symptoms of a panic attack include extreme sweating, rapid heartbeat, dizziness, and confusion. Some people having panic attacks think they're having a heart attack. Many people who suffer from anxiety have a fear of going insane.

PICA

Pica is a disorder in which people eat things that are not food. Someone with pica might feel the need to eat dirt, paper, or chalk.

TOURETTE'S SYNDROME

Tourette's syndrome can cause a person to shout words uncontrollably. Sometimes these words are insulting or inappropriate.

- EATING STRANGE THINGS
- REFUSING TO EAT
- SHOUTING INSULTS

ANOREXIA NERVOSA

Anorexia nervosa is an eating disorder. Cases have been reported as far back as the 1600s. People with anorexia believe they are overweight, though many are very thin. People with this disorder eat very little. They may refuse food altogether.

MYSTERIOUS SYMPTOMS

Modern medicine has found logical reasons for many symptoms of possession. But others cannot be explained. Believers claim this is proof that demons exist and can possess people. Skeptics have other opinions.

STRANGE SPEECH

One symptom of possession is speaking strangely. A person may speak in a strange voice or use a language he or she does not know. Believers see this as proof of possession. Skeptics think people are just speaking gibberish or repeating a conversation they overheard.

RELIGIOUS HATRED

A person thought to be possessed often has violent, angry reactions to religious items. These could be a cross or a Bible. Skeptics think people may unconsciously fake these reactions because they are convinced they are possessed by demons.

PSYCHOKINESIS

Psychokinetic events occur when objects seem to move on their own. It is thought that possessed people are able to move these objects with their minds. Skeptics blame these events on the wind or other natural explanations.

LEVITATION

One of the most convincing symptoms of possession is levitation. This is when a person seems to float in midair. Levitation is a very rare symptom. To believers, it is ultimate proof of possession. Skeptics are not so easy to convince. There are no authentic, confirmed images of a person levitating. Even if there were, skilled magicians have performed similar feats.

CHAPTER 5

EXORCISM AND CASES OF POSSESSION

Many people believe exorcisms get rid of demons. Most exorcists are Catholic priests. The Catholic church trains exorcists at special schools in Rome, Italy. Some **Protestant** ministers also perform exorcisms. They sometimes use the term deliverance ministry to describe what they are doing. Other faiths have their own ways to get rid of demons.

Protestant a Christian who does not belong to the Roman Catholic or Orthodox churches

HISTORY OF EXORCISM

The history of exorcism goes back thousands of years. Exorcisms were used in the teachings of the Hindu faith around 2,200 years ago.

In the Middle Ages, people used many different methods to perform exorcisms. In 1614 the Catholic church's Rite of Exorcism was made to establish one official method.

200 BC

AD 1614

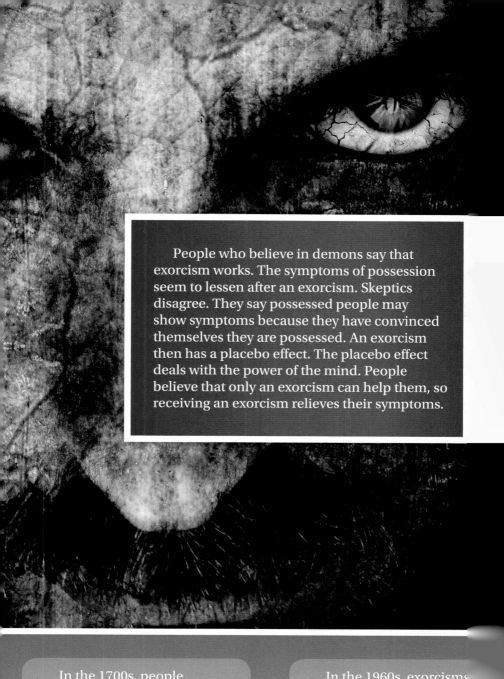

People who believe in demons say that exorcism works. The symptoms of possession seem to lessen after an exorcism. Skeptics disagree. They say possessed people may show symptoms because they have convinced themselves they are possessed. An exorcism then has a placebo effect. The placebo effect deals with the power of the mind. People believe that only an exorcism can help them, so receiving an exorcism relieves their symptoms.

In the 1700s, people turned to reason, science, and medicine. This time was called the Age of Enlightenment. The number of possession reports and exorcisms dropped.

1700S

In the 1960s, exorcisms made a comeback in some Christian churches. Leaders of these groups began to stress deliverance from the devil and demons.

1960S

THE CASE OF ROLAND DOE

In 1949 the story of a 13-year-old Maryland boy hit the newspapers. Reporters called him Roland Doe to hide his identity. According to the articles, Roland's family noticed strange happenings beginning in January. Scratching noises came from the walls. Roland's bed would shake. Pictures, fruit, and other objects would drop to the floor whenever he was near.

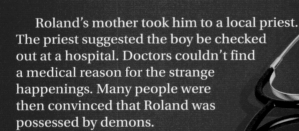

Roland's mother took him to a local priest. The priest suggested the boy be checked out at a hospital. Doctors couldn't find a medical reason for the strange happenings. Many people were then convinced that Roland was possessed by demons.

Eventually Catholic priests agreed to perform exorcisms on Roland. Witnesses reported that during the exorcisms Roland spit and acted violently. He spoke to the priests in Latin, a language he had never learned. Some witnesses claimed he had a rash on his body that spelled out words and numbers. Priests performed between 20 and 30 exorcisms on Roland before a demon was reportedly exorcised.

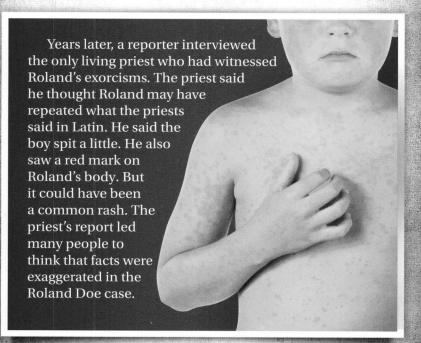

Years later, a reporter interviewed the only living priest who had witnessed Roland's exorcisms. The priest said he thought Roland may have repeated what the priests said in Latin. He said the boy spit a little. He also saw a red mark on Roland's body. But it could have been a common rash. The priest's report led many people to think that facts were exaggerated in the Roland Doe case.

THE CASE OF ANNELIESE MICHEL

Anneliese Michel was born in Germany in 1952. She grew up in a very religious family. As a teenager, she began suffering from seizures. Doctors diagnosed Anneliese with epilepsy.

By the time she was 18, Anneliese's seizures weren't her only disturbing symptoms. She began to have visions of the devil during her prayers. Anneliese told doctors that she heard demon voices telling her to do things. By 1973 Anneliese had become very depressed. She believed that she was possessed by many demons, including the demonic spirit of Adolf Hitler.

Doctors tried to relieve Anneliese's symptoms with several medications. None of them seemed to help. Eventually, Anneliese's parents requested an exorcism from the Catholic church. Their request was denied. Church officials believed Anneliese's problems were medical.

By 1975 Anneliese was acting even more strangely. She started biting and screaming at her family. She tore her clothes off and slept on the floor. Anneliese ate flies and coal. She even drank her own urine. She went around the house and destroyed religious items. At this point, the Catholic church agreed to perform exorcisms on Anneliese.

Anneliese began receiving exorcisms in September of 1975. One or two sessions were held each week. The priests recorded the exorcisms on audiotape. On the recordings, Anneliese can be heard screaming. She speaks in different voices. The priests and her parents said she was possessed by several demons. After the first few exorcisms, Anneliese's symptoms got better. But they soon returned and got even worse.

Anneliese prayed constantly for relief. Her knees became sore and bled from kneeling to pray so often. She refused to eat and became very ill. Anneliese saw visions of the Virgin Mary telling her that she would save souls through her suffering. Eventually Anneliese refused further exorcisms. Starving and very ill, Anneliese died on July 1, 1976.

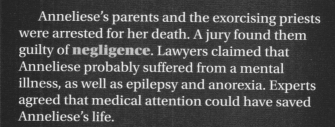

Anneliese's parents and the exorcising priests were arrested for her death. A jury found them guilty of **negligence**. Lawyers claimed that Anneliese probably suffered from a mental illness, as well as epilepsy and anorexia. Experts agreed that medical attention could have saved Anneliese's life.

Even though the courts blamed Anneliese's death on her parents and the priests, many people disagreed. They were convinced that Anneliese had indeed been possessed.

negligence   being careless or inattentive to one's responsibilities

CHAPTER 6

DEMONS IN POP CULTURE

As a college student in 1949, William Peter Blatty read about the case of Roland Doe. The story of the possessed boy fascinated him, and he never forgot it. Eventually Blatty wrote a book inspired by the event. His book, *The Exorcist*, was published in 1971. It soon became a best seller.

In 1973 *The Exorcist* was made into a movie. The public loved it. Interest in demons and exorcism rose after that. Demons had officially become part of pop culture.

FACT

The movie *The Exorcist* won two Academy Awards.

INSIDE AN EXORCISM

What happens at a Catholic exorcism is not as exciting as the movies make it seem. The rite lasts an hour or less. It consists mostly of prayer. The priest asks the demon to identify itself. The priest tries to wear down and weaken the demon with prayers. Often multiple exorcisms are performed before a person reports feeling relieved of the symptoms of possession.

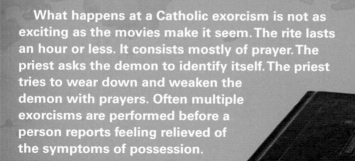

The movie *The Exorcist* remained popular with audiences for decades. In 2004 the movie *Exorcist: The Beginning* was released.

INSPIRATION FOR EMILY ROSE

The story of Roland Doe wasn't the only famous case of possession to make it into theatres. The events surrounding Anneliese Michel's death inspired a movie as well. *The Exorcism of Emily Rose* took the story out of 1970s Germany and placed it in modern-day America. The movie was a hit. Many of the facts of the case were changed. But people were still amazed that the movie was based on a true story. It caused people to consider their own beliefs in demons.

CULTURAL SOURCE HYPOTHESIS

Demons, ghosts, and vampires have made a huge splash in pop culture. These characters are portrayed as fiction in books, TV shows, and movies. But they can affect people's beliefs about reality.

The Cultural Source Hypothesis is a theory about belief in supernatural happenings. It states that popular culture can plant ideas in people's minds. These ideas affect people's experiences. For example, someone might see mist over a marsh and think it is a ghost.

In 2010 the movie *The Last Exorcism* was released. Like other exorcism movies before it, the film is said to be based on a true story.

DEMONS: FACT OR FAITH?

Demons have a solid place in pop culture. They often appear alongside witches and vampires. But very few people actually believe in the existence of witches and vampires. Why then, do many people still believe in demons?

↗ **VAMPIRE**

↗ **WITCH**

↗ **DEMON**

Many religions teach that demons are real and must be cast out. Faithful religious followers believe these teachings. But skeptics see no evidence for demons. What do you believe?

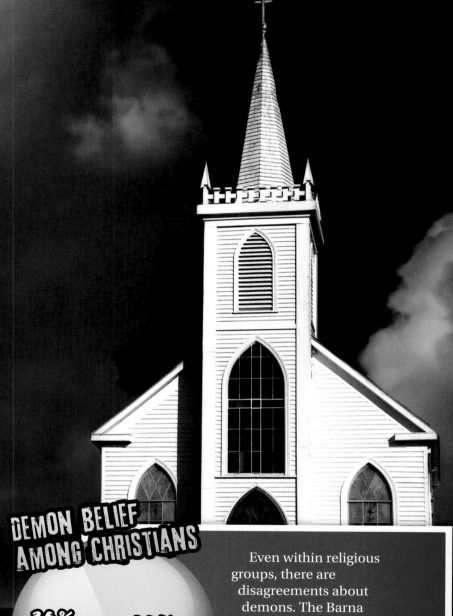

DEMON BELIEF AMONG CHRISTIANS

36% don't believe

64% believe

Even within religious groups, there are disagreements about demons. The Barna Group polled 1,800 American Christians in 2009. Sixty-four percent of them believed people could be influenced by demons.

GLOSSARY

cannibal (KA-nuh-buhl)—a person who eats other people

divine (duh-VYN)—to do with or from God or a god

exorcism (EKS-uhr-sizz-uhm)—a religious ritual that is supposed to cast out a demon from a person's mind or body

hallucination (huh-loo-suh-NAY-shuhn)—something seen or heard that is not really there

negligence (NEG-luh-juhnss)—being careless or inattentive to one's responsibilities

paralyze (PAIR-uh-lize)—to make someone or something helpless or unable to function

possessed (poh-ZEST)—having one's mind and body taken over

Protestant (PROT-uh-stuhnt)—a Christian who does not belong to the Roman Catholic or Orthodox churches

psychic (SYE-kik)—having the ability to sense, see, or hear things that others do not

seizure (SEE-zhur)—a sudden shaking spasm that may include other symptoms

shaman (SHAH-man)—a religious or spiritual leader

skeptic (SKEP-tik)—a person who questions things that other people believe in

supernatural (soo-per-NACH-ur-uhl)—something that cannot be given an ordinary explanation

unconscious (uhn-KON-shuhss)—describes something done without the person doing it being aware

READ MORE

Blohm, Craig E. *The Possessed.* Mysterious Encounters. Detroit: KidHaven Press, 2008.

Ganeri, Anita. *Demons and Ghouls.* The Dark Side. New York: PowerKids Press, 2011.

Hamilton, S. L. *Ghosts.* Xtreme Monsters. Edina, Minn.: ABDO Publishing Company, 2011.

INTERNET SITES

FactHound offers a safe, fun way to find Internet sites related to this book. All of the sites on FactHound have been researched by our staff.

Here's all you do:

Visit *www.facthound.com*

Type in this code: 9781429648158

INDEX